To Maxime, Camille, and Paul Daniel
Special thanks to Lucie Schmitt

Series Editors:

Laure Mistral
Philippe Godard

Also Available:

We Live in India
We Live in China
We Live in Japan

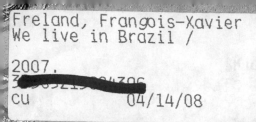

Kids Around the World

François-Xavier Freland

Illustrations by Sophie Duffet

Brasil

We live in

Brazil

Abrams Books for Young Readers
New York

Atlantic Ocean

VENEZUELA
GUYANA
SURINAME
FRENCH GUYANA
COLOMBIA

Roraima
Amapá

Amazon River
Amazonas
Pará

Maranhão
Ceará
Rio Grand do Norte
Paraíba
Piauí
Pernambuco
Alagoas
Sergipe

Acre
PERU
Rondônia
Tocantins
Bahia

Mato Grosso

BOLIVIA
Brasília
Goiás
Salvador

Minas Gerais
Espírito Santo

Mato Grosso do Sul
São Paulo
Rio de Janeiro
Rio de Janeiro

CHILE
PARAGUAY
Paraná
São Paulo
Santa Catarina

ARGENTINA

Rio Grande do Sul

URUGUAY

North
Center West
Northeast
Southeast
South

B r a z i l

A Look at Today's Brazil

Brazil is a federal republic made up of twenty-six federated states. Individual states have significant autonomy in specific areas.

Surface area: 3.3 million square miles. Brazil covers nearly half of South America.

Population: 178 million; 57 people per square mile.

Ethnicity: 53 percent white, 38 percent multiracial (persons with parents of different backgrounds), 6 percent black, 1 percent Asian, 1 percent Amerindian, 1 percent unspecified.

Religions: 80 percent Catholic, 7 percent Protestant, 13 percent miscellaneous religions (roughly a hundred sects).

Official language: Portuguese.

Main cities: Brasília, the political capital (population 2 million); São Paulo, the financial and economic capital (population 18.4 million, suburbs included); Rio de Janeiro, the cultural capital (population 11.1 million, suburbs included); Salvador da Bahia (2.5 million, suburbs included).

Geographical features: sweeping plains in the north where the Amazon River and its tributaries flow; in the south, hills and eroded mountains.

Climate: mostly tropical; relatively high temperatures year-round and heavy precipitation. Southern Brazil, however, has seasons that are nearly as varied as those in Europe. Northern Brazil's dry season runs from June to August, and its rainy season is the rest of the year.

Agriculture: Brazil produces an array of products, but mainly sugarcane, coffee, cacao, soy, maize, manioc, plus a wide range of fruits. Brazil also produces beef.

Raw materials: ranks second in the world for iron production.

Currency: the *real* is Brazil's money.

This Is Brazil

Let's take a trip back in time. Let's go back five hundred years to when the first Europeans were just beginning to explore the Americas.

One night in the year 1500, Portuguese navigator Pedro Álvares Cabral stood on his ship's deck, lifted his spyglass, and noticed the cross-shaped constellation called Santa Cruz pointing to the unexplored shoreline of this land. He immediately named the territory Terra da Santa Cruz (the Land of the Holy Cross). At the time, a few Amerindian tribes (the Tupi and the Guarani, to name two) lived there peacefully on the Atlantic coast. Soon thereafter, Portuguese colonists began pouring in to exploit the seemingly endless resources of this vast territory: sugarcane and wood. Amerindian tribesmen were recruited to exploit these riches. Those who refused to obey were severely punished.

Around the middle of the sixteenth century, the name changed from Terra da Santa Cruz to Brazil. The new name came from *pau brasil*, a prized hardwood called brazilwood in English. The tree grows abundantly in the northwestern Pernambuco area. Once dry, the wood takes a ruddy tint, like burning embers. *Brasil* in Portuguese means "embers."

The Portuguese soon began shipping in slaves from Angola and Guinea in Africa to perform the hard labor on their plantations in Brazil. By 1550, the first groups of enslaved Africans had landed in the port of Salvador da Bahia. Bahia became the capital of the territory, desired by many world powers. France and the Netherlands tried but failed several times to colonize Brazil. Through the centuries, Brazil has become a world power. It gained its independence from Portugal in 1822.

After World War II, Brazil experienced an economic boom. The war had severely affected Europe, and Brazil started exporting food and raw materials that Europeans desperately needed. Starting in the 1950s, Brazil's development soared. In 1956, the new president, Juscelino

Kubitschek de Oliveira, decided to turn Brazil into a modern nation. His slogan was "fifty years in five years." He wanted Brazil to leap ahead to make up for lagging behind in the industrial race.

In 1960, the brand-new city of Brasília was complete. Located in the heart of the nation, this city was designed to be the political and administrative capital. Unfortunately, the dream of an advanced, modern nation came to an end in 1964. The country was run by a series of military dictators until 1985.

Democracy did return, however. Free elections were held. A parliament composed of a Chamber of Deputies and a Senate was elected. Today, despite the nation's vast wealth, Brazil is a country with terrible social inequalities. More than 35 million Brazilians (nearly one in five inhabitants) live in poverty.

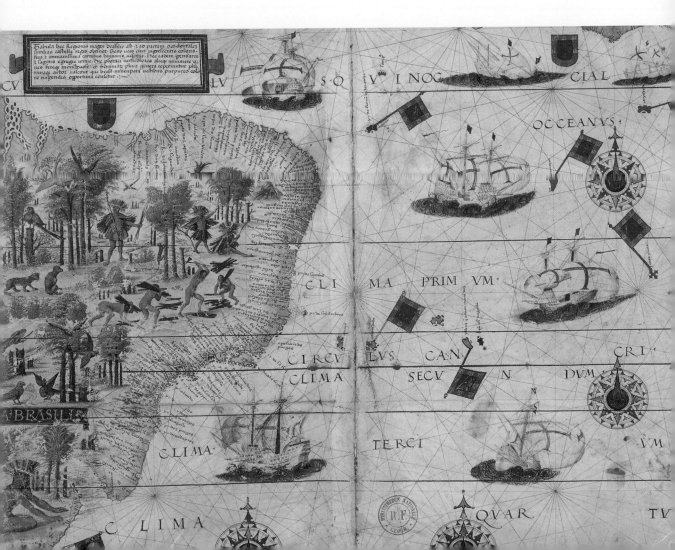

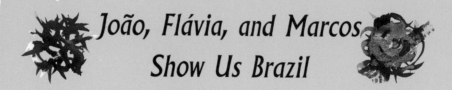

João, Flávia, and Marcos
Show Us Brazil

In this book, we are going to explore Brazil's many regions with three children.

Meet João. He is ten years old and comes from an interracial family. He lives in Salvador da Bahia. Coming from a poor family, João doesn't always have it so easy. As young as he is, he has to work to help out his family. But you would never guess it from his smile! Salvador da Bahia is a colorful and festive city. The sky is usually bright blue and the houses are painted vibrant colors. Music can be heard everywhere, and it is not uncommon to see dancing in the streets. The city is lots of fun.

Flávia lives in Brasília, the capital, an amazing city that was built from the ground up in the late 1950s. Flávia is a bright student. She loves to travel. She and her family usually take trips through the Amazon rainforest on vacation.

Marcos is a young boy of twelve who lives in a rich neighborhood of Rio de Janeiro. The city is famous for its sunshine, beaches, and carnival. It is a gigantic combination of metropolis and sea resort. It is located in the southeast corner of the country on the Atlantic coast.

João, the Boy from Bahia

As boys' names go, João is just as common in Brazil as its equivalent in English-speaking countries. Can you guess what it is? Yes, it's John! Ten-year-old João's family lives in Salvador da Bahia, in the region called *Nordeste* ("Northeast" in English). It is an arid region prone to droughts. Like many Brazilians in this area, João's parents are poor. Although he is just a boy, he has to help them by working, too.

Salvador da Bahia, or Bahia, as many people call it, is a former capital city of Brazil. It was founded by the Portuguese in 1549. It is one of the prettiest cities in South America. The sugarcane industry made it a wealthy market town. Today, beautiful palaces covered in *azulejos* are evidence of a bygone period of luxury and splendor. *Azulejos* are tiny decorative earthenware or porcelain squares. They have hand-painted pictures on them. People hang them all around their windows and doors. Salvador da Bahia also boasts magnificent baroque churches with luminous façades painted in cheerful pastels: reds, yellows, and blues. Contrary to the cold, gray churches many North Americans and Europeans are accustomed to, places of worship in Bahia try to attract passersby. They have intriguing ornaments, sculptures, and molding.

"Fitas, fitas! Muito baratas! Dois reais!" ("Ribbons, ribbons! Very inexpensive. Two reais!")

João calls out this morning to people in the streets of Pelourinho, an old quarter of the city. He is selling *fitas*, which are small good-luck ribbons. They come in all colors. People generally wear them around their wrists. Pelourinho is one of the city's most charming historic areas. It attracts many tourists. It is chock-full of restaurants and bars where musicians play.

◉ The Pulse of Africa Beats in Bahia

Bahia is mainly a port. Its economic development sprang from slave trading. For centuries, men and women were plucked from their homelands in Africa to work here.

Once, the Pelourinho quarter was crowded with slaves who would be sold or auctioned off to slave masters, many of whom had few scruples. Most slaves were sent to work on area plantations, but others became household servants. As the centuries passed, the African presence became an essential part of the fabric of the city, and the city became known as the Black Pearl of Brazil.

Slavery was abolished in 1888, more than a century ago. Since then, Bahia has preserved its African influence. Like children from many other families, João is half black and half white. His father is from a long line of Portuguese merchants. His mother comes from a black family originally from Guinea. It is often said that Bahia is the meeting point for Amazonian Indians, the descendants of Portuguese colonists, and the descendants of black slaves.

João often can be found at the Jorge Amado Foundation. Amado, who died in 2001, was a writer. He actively defended black rights, giving these long-oppressed people added pride. João knows this place quite well. While selling souvenirs to tourists who gather in front of the building, João became friends with Flavio, the museum attendant. Thanks to Flavio, João enjoys frequent free visits to the museum. Sometimes he finishes his workday in the video-viewing room watching a film based on one of Amado's novels. Because João cannot read very well (he dropped out of school some time ago), video is the best way for him to appreciate Amado's poetry.

João has decided to take his time this morning. When he walks past the museum, Flavio greets him as he pulls open the heavy wooden doors.

"Bom dia, João. Como vai hoje?" ("Hello, João. How are you today?")
"Oi, velho Flavio. Bem e você?" ("Hi, old Flavio. I'm fine, and you?")
"Beleza!" ("Very well!")
"Até mais, Flavio!" ("See you later, Flavio!")

João is now walking on the old, slippery, paved streets of Bahia. He knows the city like the back of his hand. He often shuttles back and forth from the Pelourinho neighborhood to the docks where boats ferry tourists to and from the island of Itaparica, across the bay. When he glances at the neighborhood up the hill, Pelourinho looks like it is clinging to the hillside. As João strolls by the arts-and-crafts market near the harbor, he stops to watch a capoeira demonstration.

Capoeira: Symbol of Black Brazilians' Struggle

Capoeira originally began as a martial art that was disguised to look like a dance. It was invented by slaves. They honed and perfected it during the three centuries that they were exploited by the Portuguese Brazilians. The choreography of the dance is steeped in African dance traditions, but it also gives people combat training.

The dance was invented in the prisons of Bahia, where slaves were locked up before being handed over to their masters. Although the slaves would say they were exercising to keep in shape, they were secretly engaging in combat training. The seemingly ordinary moves are, in fact, attack moves. A prison guard opening a door might unexpectedly find himself caught in a flurry of punches, kicks, and chops. Some say the art helped thousands of slaves to escape from jails.

It is hardly surprising, then, that capoeira was illegal until 1937. Today, it is considered a martial art in its own right. Ten million people practice the sport in Brazil. Second only to soccer, capoeira is Brazil's most popular sport. But it's popular not only in Brazil. Its popularity has extended around the world. It is now practiced in more than ninety countries.

Generally, two young men dressed in white face off in the center of the *roda* (circle) formed by the other dancers who sing and set the rhythm as the *berimbau* sets the mood for the dancers. The *berimbau* is a single-string percussion instrument that looks like a bow attached to a gourd. It makes a loud bass sound. The songs are intended to instruct the combatants. The fighters imitate reptiles, felines, and apes. For example, they swing a leg over their adversary's head and imitate the slashing of lion claws. In this sport, there are no real winners. What matters most is showing great mastery of body, mind, and spirit through a series of powerful, rapid, and gracefully executed moves.

◉ A Boy and His Music

João leaves the capoeira dancers and returns to his business. In the space of three hours, he has sold two dozen *fitas*.

He returns to the Pelourinho quarter for a moment's rest at Praça da Sé, a nice square where he can relax and play his *cavaquinho*, a small guitarlike instrument that he often has strapped on his back. João made his own. He took four boards and four strings and put them together. Sometimes, when he plays in the streets, people toss him coins. But João refuses to take them because, for him, music is sacred. It is not for sale.

Music is everywhere in Bahia. It is often said that Bahia is Brazil's music capital. Just about everyone there has a musical inclination. João's maternal grandfather, whom he calls Avô Basilio (Grandpa Basilio), told him Guinean drums still beat in their hearts. His grandfather taught him the basics of playing the *cavaquinho*, and João enjoys strumming Bahia melodies with his grandfather in local cafés on Sundays.

Two or three times a year, he and Avô Basilio return to the family village in the heart of the Sertão, a poor and arid region near Bahia. João likes the peaceful atmosphere. He likes to plop down on his old uncles' cushions and listen to them. The family get-togethers are great opportunities to improvise and play *forró* (folk music) late into the night.

After his half-hour break, João returns to the restaurant-lined street to eat at his grandmother's place. He crosses himself as he passes São Francisco church. It is his way of thanking God for the *fitas* he sold that morning. João's family is very religious. In fact, they have two religions.

Like his parents, João was baptized in the Catholic religion, but they also participate in *Candomblé*.

◉ Candomblé: *An Encounter with the Spirits*

*C*andomblé is a centuries-old Brazilian religion with African roots.

Ripped from their families and homelands, black slaves lost everything except their traditions and their beliefs. Although the Portuguese missionaries converted the slaves to Catholicism once they arrived in Brazil, ancestral traditions were kept alive with *Candomblé*. The religion was banned for a very long time by Brazilian law. Authorities looked

15

down on it and considered it to be little more than a hodgepodge of superstitions and occult practices bordering on witchcraft. This was because, in reality, they feared that the religious gatherings might turn into organized revolts.

João occasionally attends one of the possession rituals called *ebo*. The priest or priestess implores the help of the divinities, the *orixás*, to resolve problems that a person or a clan is having. Today, ceremonies take place as discretely as possible, behind houses, on the edge of town, in yards specially set up as places of worship and long kept secret for fear of repression.

Today, the ceremonies are not outlawed. They are acknowledged as expressions of faith. The rituals help believers enter trances. A choir and a percussion band provide the music. The faithful sing and clap their hands while the "sons and daughters of the saints" dance barefoot. They spin around and around. The twirling eventually sends them into a trance. At this point, many begin speaking in the name of the divinity, through the voice of the Exu, the spirit of the dead. They believe the Exu is an intermediary between the visible and the invisible worlds, a messenger spirit who transmits the words of the *orixás* through the mouths of the sons and daughters of the saints.

◉ Orixás: *Spiriting Believers to Inner Peace*

O*rixás*, as the divine spirits are called, have specific duties.

In general, *orixás* protect believers in specific areas of life. For example, fishermen should pray to Iemanja, the goddess of the sea. Omulu, the master of health, provides protection against disease. Then there is Oxum, the goddess of beauty and seduction, who answers prayers about matters of love. For each believer, there is at least one god, or patron spirit, looking over him or her.

João is a *filho de Xango* (son of Xango), one of the most powerful *orixás*. Xango is the god of lightning and thunder. He can easily be recognized by the war hatchet over his head. Xango has been his family's spirit for generations, as he gives strength to work. Beside his little silver cross necklace hangs a medal of Xango, João's patron spirit. Having two religions is perfectly natural in João's family, as well as many other Brazilian families.

⬤ Cooking, Bahia Style!

João sees his grandmother working at her kitchen-on-wheels at the end of Gregorio de Matos Street. She feeds him every day. João doesn't complain, because her cooking is beyond compare. Everyone in Bahia comes to taste her delicious recipes.

For nearly forty years, every morning Avó Miralva (João's grandmother) has set up her portable stove on the pavement. Customers begin showing up at lunchtime. They stand around enjoying her excellent *acarajés*, made from deep-fried white-bean mash that she usually slices in two and stuffs with shrimp and a vegetable mix of tomatoes, zucchini, and okra (a long, pointy, and fuzzy fruit that is cooked like a vegetable).

When she has the time, Avó Miralva tells her cooking secrets to João. She teaches him where various herbs and spices come from and how to use them in preparing food. He knows that her cooking oil comes from the *dendê*, a palm tree native to equatorial Africa. The oil has a distinctly bitter odor and flavor. It is widely used in local cuisine. João likes watching his grandmother sitting on her stool, dressed all in white, stirring her sauces and patting ingredients together in the hollow of her hand with precise and methodical movements.

One day, while visiting the Afro-Brazilian Museum, João saw old frescoes illustrating scenes from African life. There in the wall paintings, he thought he recognized his own grandmother among the women in traditional clothing, also cooking on the ground, over wood fires outside their huts. One day, if the gods grant him his wish, João would very much like to cross the ocean to retrace the steps of his ancestors and bring back more recipes as a gift for his grandmother.

Meanwhile, he enjoys a few of her *acarajés* before returning to work. Although his job can sometimes be tiring, and certainly limits his free time, João has a real sense of freedom when he strolls through the streets of this cheerful and colorful city. People speak to each other from house to house. Everyone takes the time to live with the charming southern ambiance that Jorge Amado's books describe well.

Flávia's Expedition Through the Amazon Rainforest

Flávia is eleven years old and lives in Brasília, the political and administrative capital of Brazil. This city, full of futurist architecture, was built in the span of just four years. It was inaugurated in 1960. The district of Brasília is surrounded by the state of Goiás, located pretty much in the center of Brazil. Brasília is where Brazil's president and the rest of the members of the federal government live and work.

Flávia is very proud to be from the capital. Her parents' home is right beside the Lago do Paranoá, a human-made lake. Her parents moved here in 1981. They found an apartment that is only steps away from their jobs at the Tourism Ministry. Standing on the balcony of their apartment, Flávia and her parents have a sweeping view of the city. Despite their relatively low salaries as civil servants (her mother is a secretary and her father is in communications), their home is spacious, modern, and very comfortable. In the 1980s, the government offered low rents to encourage people to move to Brasília.

◉ Brasília: An Old Dream That Came True

A nineteenth-century priest named Dom João Bosco predicted that in the third millennium a new city would be built deeper inland. The place he predicted was close to where Brasília was eventually built. It was only in 1956 that President Juscelino Kubitschek de Oliveira decided to make the old dream come true. Kubitschek de Oliveira was an ambitious man with a vision. He was also a native son of the poorer hinterland and knew the importance of placing the brand-new capital in the heart of the nation.

For four years, thousands of construction workers and machines labored to tame this arid desert plateau at an altitude of 3,600 feet. The idea was to center and balance this vast country for both administrative and political reasons. Most of Brazil's inhabitants live on the coast. The largest cities dot the Atlantic shoreline: Belém, Recife, Salvador da Bahia, Rio de Janeiro, and São Paulo are all either on or very close to the coast.

At the time Brasília was being built, the nation's economic development looked very promising. The country was becoming aware of its immense natural resources. Petrobras, a public corporation for petroleum production, was founded in 1955. The Brazilian government had a plan. It was determined to stimulate the economy elsewhere in the country, particularly in the state of Goiás, known for its poverty.

Viewed from the sky, Brasília is a cross-shaped city that looks a lot like the outline of a gigantic airplane. Seen from the ground, the city appears very futuristic. It looks like an extraterrestrial city, with its monuments shaped like flying saucers! Flávia's father often quotes what the famous

Russian cosmonaut Yuri Gagarin said on his first visit to Brasília: "It feels like I've landed on another planet!"

Today, Brasília has a population of 1.5 million. Brasília's urban planners, Lucio Costa and Oscar Niemeyer, had only imagined a population of 500,000. But during the 1960s, Brazil's population increased significantly and, at the same time, began moving into urbanized areas. Today, eight out of every ten Brazilians live in a city. Furthermore, thousands of poor peasants flocked to the center of Brazil and toward Brasília in hopes of finding decent-paying jobs.

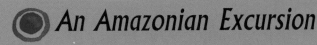

● An Amazonian Excursion

Despite its immense human-made lake, its parks, and its gardens, Brasília really heats up in the summer. The capital sits on a vast desert plateau. There is hardly any shade or wind to bring temperatures down.

Today is a big departure day. Flávia and her family have planned to spend the school holiday in the Amazon rainforest. It will be cooler there. They will take a cruise on the Amazon River. They started preparing their Kombi several weeks ago. Kombis are very popular and very practical vehicles in Brazil. Outfitted as camping vans, they have mattresses, stoves, and lots of cupboards for stowing things. Like buses, they are an inexpensive way of traveling through this vast land, but they allow you to do it on your schedule, not on a bus schedule.

Flávia's family first drives out through the northern section of the city. Flávia is sitting in the back with her brother Marcio and sister

23

Ana. To reach the Trans-Amazonian Highway, they have to take the freeway that cuts through the city. Everyone is in a very festive mood. They already feel they have left their worries behind. With each monument they pass, they realize that there is much of the city that they do not regularly see. This is hardly surprising, as the city is so spread out. Flávia asks her parents about the city's intriguing monuments.

"What's that?" Flávia asks, pointing to an odd building with a tower and two round white structures on either side.

"That's Three-Powers Square," her mother replies. "Look at the two buildings. One is upside down and the other is right-side up. They represent the balance of powers. First there is the legislative branch of government, which makes laws. Then there is the executive branch (the president). And the third is the judiciary branch, which ensures that the laws are served with justice. Without the balance of powers, there could be no democracy, Flávia."

◉ Dictatorship Wedges Its Way In

In the early 1960s, Brasília symbolized Brazil's good fortune.

The economy was in full swing. The standard of living had improved greatly. The country had upgraded its infrastructure, and the people were eating well. Brazil had opened up to the world. It was showing its exuberance for life with its carnival, its beaches, and its entrancing, rhythmic music.

However, only a few years later, storm clouds had gathered on the horizon. In 1964, the army toppled the government and took over. The coup d'état (overthrow of the government) put a military dictatorship in place. The nation was sent spiraling into a period of repression. Opponents of the regime were arrested or assassinated. Political parties were banned. The press was censored. Democracy did not return until the 1980s, after long labor strikes that paralyzed the nation and enormous antigovernment demonstrations that took place nationwide. The first free presidential election in twenty years was held in 1985.

The Kombi has now covered over 430 miles on the northward-bound highway. Brasília is long behind them. Flávia presses her head against the window and watches the sun set on the seemingly endless savannah. These vast arid plains were once grassy. Big irrigation systems have since transformed them into fields of soy, corn, and cattle ranches.

These photos are of political dissidents who disappeared during the dictatorship.

These are the plains where Flávia's grandparents used to live. They had a small farm of only a few acres.

They had to work very hard to make a living. After several very bad harvests, they had to pack up and leave. They now live in one of Brasília's suburbs. Fortunately for them, all of their children have successful careers and are able to take care of them financially.

As the 1950s brought greater mechanization, *fazendas* (large farms with nearly 2,500 acres) started squeezing out the smaller farms. The competition was too much for small-time farmers. Many farmers couldn't read and were poorly informed about the benefits of modern techniques such as fertilizing and the use of pesticides. As a result, they went bankrupt and had to sell their land. Others were forced off their land. Having lost everything, they moved to poor towns on the edges of big cities. A few brave souls tried to occupy land suitable for farming even if it meant confrontation with the owners and the law.

Their dire situations spawned the *sem terras* (landless people). The ruin of the small farmer spread from the north to the south, through the Amazon basin and down toward the Mato Grosso. It gradually affected farmers all over the country. Despite government intervention, nothing has successfully curbed rural poverty.

The following day, late in the evening, after an exhausting day of travel (nearly 950 miles in just two days!), Flávia and her family finally arrive in Belém in a heavy downpour. There, they board a double-decker riverboat bound for Manaus, the capital of the Amazon.

Belém is a major port city located at the mouth of the Amazon River, very close to where it flows into the ocean. All the merchandise and material (mainly timber and rubber) produced in the rainforest regions passes through this port. Given its location, Belém is also one of the wettest cities in Brazil. The evaporation of water in the steamy Amazonian rainforest triggers frequent showers over the surrounding area. In and around Belém, it rains anywhere from one hundred to two hundred fifty days a year! Humidity can easily reach 90 percent.

The Amazon River is 3,900 miles long. It is the world's second-longest river. It has the planet's highest volume of water for a river. Imagine three billion gallons of water per minute flowing past Belém just moments before gushing into the Atlantic.

Not long after dawn, the echo of footsteps and voices outside the van wakes Flávia. The ferry is approaching a village. Some of the passengers gather their bags and suitcases. They stand on the deck, preparing to land. Flávia looks over the rail and notices snoozing crocodiles along the riverbanks a hundred yards ahead. As the boat approaches, the beasts dart into the water. Actually, they are *jacarés*, somewhat smaller than their African cousins, the crocodiles—if you can call seven feet long small. Her father tells her that deeper in the forest, there are jaguars and all kinds of serpents and poisonous spiders.

The Amazon Rainforest: Wealth and Health

The biggest forest on this planet is Brazil's rainforest. The Amazon rainforest covers nine of Brazil's states and accounts for 60 percent of Brazil's surface. It is the least populated area of the nation. Only 20 million people live there.

It is also a difficult region to reach. It has very few roads. Several zones of the rainforest are internationally protected zones, because they are home to a multitude of plant and animal species. Five hundred mammal species have been counted thus far. There are more than four hundred reptile species. More than three thousand species of fish populate the rivers in the Amazonian region.

The Amazon rainforest is also home to numerous rare birds. Among them are the hummingbirds with

their multicolored feathers, and the magnificent toucans. The toucan's long orange or yellow beak and its white-and-black feathers are impressive. Toucans are prone to temper tantrums. They may squawk loudly and give you a bit of a scare, but it is all for show. Toucans should not be confused with parrots. The most popular parrot is the *ara macao*. It has beautiful blue-and-yellow wings. Both toucans and parrots enjoy human company. They like to sit on people's shoulders and can be quite affectionate.

One evening, Flávia strolls out to the front of the deck. Over the humming of the engine, she believes she can hear strange animal noises. It might be something wild stalking the riverbank, she thinks. And she is right. She notices a boy on the deck who is also intrigued by the noise. Suddenly, he points excitedly to a tapir in the tall grass. At six feet long, tapirs are fairly large forest animals. They look like a cross between a pig and a hippo. The boy's name is Yanoki. He is a member of the Yanomami tribe, an ancient Indian nation that lives north of Manaus along the border with Venezuela. Yanoki and his father are returning home after selling handcrafts in a Belém market.

The Yanomami and Other Amazonian Natives

There are roughly forty different tribes of people native to the Amazon rainforest. Their total population today is only 200,000.

But in the sixteenth century, at the time of the Europeans' conquest of the Americas, their population was estimated at six to seven million. Whole nations were wiped out either by wars to grab their land or by diseases that the Westerners had brought with them.

Amazonian Amerindians have preserved their traditional way of life. Many still live in remote villages, far from cities and towns. They generally live in small straw huts—rudimentary, fragile buildings. The ultra-modern satellite dishes on their traditional roofs look out of place.

In the middle of the village, you will usually find a building larger than all the others. It serves as community center and temple. The local shaman (medicine man) performs healing rituals there to free those afflicted by illnesses or evil spirits.

Amerindians in this region have knowledge of many fascinating subjects. They include not only knowledge of medicinal plants, but of the universe. The Tembes tribe invented their own astronomy. They live in the northeast portion of the rainforest. They discovered numerous constellations and gave them fanciful names. Take, for example, the Hummingbird constellation. It reminds you of the tiny bird with the long beak. When it appears in the sky, it heralds the start of the rainy season. The dry season is heralded by the arrival of the Emu constellation. Emus are big birds that are similar to ostriches. Various communities set up rituals to salute the Emu constellation, for it marks the beginning of the harvest season. Unfortunately, most of the Amerindian communities such as the Nambikwaras, the Bororos, the Caiapos, and the Waimiri-Atroaris (many of whom have cultural heritages dating back a thousand years) are faced with a threat to their existence since a devastating plague has hit the Amazon region—deforestation.

Natural Imbalance

Beginning in 1972, military dictators built roads into and through the Amazon rainforest in order to connect the region with the rest of the country. These highways have had disastrous effects.

The monumental road construction project attracted loggers and gold miners. They have devastated the Amazon forest and continue to do so. According to recent estimates, some 90 million acres of forest have vanished. At this rate, the Amazon rainforest could vanish by the year 2020.

The plague of forest fires that came with the construction and mining also means more gas emissions, thus heightening the greenhouse effect, in which gases trapped in the atmosphere cause the global temperature to rise. The result would be detrimental to all life on Earth.

Scientists observing the growing occurrence of droughts in the region over recent years agree. The massive deforestation in the Amazon, the planet's last great tropical jungle, has had a huge impact on global warming. This climate change is causing polar ice to melt; this in turn will spur torrential precipitation, perhaps even giant tidal waves.

The trees of the forest are now being replaced by soy, a crop that disrupts the natural balance of this region. Brazil has become the second-largest soy producer, ranking right after the United States. The impact of the new agriculture will accelerate the extinction of certain plants unique to the rainforest environment. And this change in the food chain will likely cause several animal species to go extinct for lack of nourishment. Besides the terrible consequences for the environment, the unchecked deforestation has a very human cost, too.

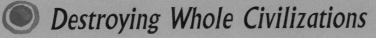

Destroying Whole Civilizations

For some local tribes, like the Yanomami, deforestation has had a major impact. For them, it has been devastating.

Slicing north to south through the rainforest, the extension of the Trans-Amazonian Highway has endangered the small Yanomami tribe. Before the road was built, their region was totally inaccessible and hidden. Without realizing what they were doing, gold miners pouring into the area in the 1980s brought deadly diseases with them. The tribe had never been exposed to yellow fever and had certainly never been vaccinated. They were overwhelmed by the loss of community leaders and temples, and the destruction of whole villages.

Today, the government seems to be paying attention to their plight. The international community has pressured Brazil to acknowledge the existence of the Yanomami and to grant them their own territory. In the 1990s, Brazilian courts found a few gold diggers guilty of the genocide of the Yanomami.

Marcos the Carioca

Marcos is twelve. He is a Carioca. What is a Carioca? It is someone who lives in Rio de Janeiro, the *Cidade Maravilhosa* (the Marvelous City), as it is often called. Rio is certainly one of the most beautiful cities in the world. It has long beaches of white sand, and bright green mountains with steep slopes and rounded tops.

Eleven million people, suburbs included, live in Rio de Janeiro. It is also one of the most densely populated areas of the world. Wealthy people live in the low-lying areas of the city and poorer people live in the heights. Marcos lives in Ipanema, very close to Lake Freitas. Ipanema is one of the richest areas of Rio. It faces the ocean. Marcos's father is an architect and his mother runs a home-furnishing shop.

Sports: What Life in Rio Is All About

Today is Sunday and Marcos is planning to meet up with his friends on the beach. They will go to Arpoador, at the far end of Ipanema, to go surfing.

In Rio, physical exercise is very popular. Many Cariocas pay close attention to their looks because, in sunny Rio, everyone wants to look beautiful! Rich or poor, everyone spends lots of time on the beach playing in the water and tanning. You can see Carioca guys strutting up and down the beach, hoping their good looks will attract the girls' attention.

The beaches of Rio have excellent sand for playing barefoot sports like beach volleyball. The waves and currents are perfect for surfing and other water sports. Marcos enjoys surfing very much. He surfs all week whether school is in or not. In Rio, the weather is warm all year round. The school day starts at 7:00 A.M. and ends shortly after lunch at 3:00 P.M. This leaves lots of time for extracurricular activities.

All day long, boys and girls—but mostly boys—work on building and toning up muscle before they go splashing in the waves. Their favorite place to surf is at the end of a cove where shifting winds blow. Brazilian surfing started on Arpoador Beach in the 1950s. But according to some people, the first surfer was an American visiting Rio in 1928. He reportedly surfed on a cedarwood board.

Things have changed a lot since then. Dozens of shops on the beach sell expensive, sophisticated equipment. Wood boards are a thing of the past! In Rio de Janeiro, people learn to surf at a young age. There are lots of seven- and eight-year-old children with a real passion for surfing. They are generally more interested in thrills than skills.

Before meeting up with his friends on Arpoador Beach, Marcos drops in at a concession stand on the beach for some refreshing coconut milk. In Rio, fruit juice vendors are a common sight.

◉ Stunning Tropical Fruit

Brazil produces more fruit than almost any other country in the world. Brazil's 34 million tons a year include an amazing thirty-five varieties.

Many stores in Europe and the United States sell Brazilian mangoes, watermelons, apples, and oranges. But there are many other kinds of fruit. The Amazon rainforest offers lots of fruits, nuts, and berries that few of us will ever see or taste.

Fortunately for us, tropical fruits do make it to our markets, so we can enjoy them. From the state of Pará, we get the Brazil nut (also called butternut, cream nut, or *castanea*). The *açai* will give you a real boost of energy. And tiny acerolas are packed with vitamin C. They look like small cherries. The mangosteen has thick purple skin, but peel it back and inside is an all-white pulp. Delicious! *Sapotes*, or sapodillas, are egg-shaped and have scruffy brown skin when they are ripe. They taste like pears or crunchy brown sugar. Cut open the carambola, or starfruit as it is called, and you will see the amazing star shape. Squeeze any of these fruits and you get excellent juice! People in Rio drink fruit juice at all hours of the day, so it is an easy habit to pick up if you visit. In Rio, there is absolutely nothing odd about sticking a straw into a cool, refreshing coconut and walking around as you drink it. Vendors are everywhere, and they generally keep coconuts in the refrigerator. But how does anyone slice open a coconut? It is nearly as hard as steel! It takes a steady hand and a big, heavy, machete-like knife to do the job.

Marcos walks over to a vendor's stand. The barman gives him a big smile and talks to him, but keeps a close eye on the soccer game on the portable television set on the bar. Few things are more important to a Brazilian than soccer. A gust of wind may make the antenna sway and disturb the reception, but a true fan won't mind. It's the game that counts. All the more so if Rio's Flamengo team is playing against its rival team, the Fluminense.

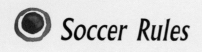

◉ Soccer Rules

Soccer is practically a religion in Rio, and in the rest of Brazil, too. Seleção is the nation's team.

When Seleção plays, the whole country holds its breath during the ninety-minute game. Each victory sends millions of Cariocas into the streets to celebrate. TV newscasts generally give soccer twenty solid minutes of airtime a day. The players' every move and deed are reported by the press. The city of Rio de Janeiro alone has four soccer teams. Their names are Botafogo, Flamengo, Fluminense, and Vasco. Each Carioca roots for his or her favorite team, which has generally been the family's favorite for generations.

Marcos's grandfather has always been a fan of the famous Clube de Regatas do Flamengo. The team's colors are red and black. Fluminense is its main rival. Marcos is not as interested in soccer as his father or his grandfather, but he does regularly go see games. Surfing is what Marcos likes most, though he does enjoy kicking the ball around on the beach with his friends. They can play for hours and hours. They often play in the late afternoon and until sunset, when the air cools and the humidity lifts. Marcos is often seen with family or friends at Maracanã stadium. It is the world's largest! It was built in 1950 for the World Cup in Brazil. Legendary players like Pelé, "the king," have played here. Pelé scored some of the most beautiful goals in soccer history. He scored his thousandth goal in the stadium in 1969. Despite rampant rumors, the 250,000-seat stadium will not be torn down. The city has classified it as a protected site.

Marcos smiles, says thanks, then continues on his way with his drink in one hand and his surfboard safely tucked under an arm. Taking the beachside walkway is a bit like floating between two worlds. On one side, you have the beach with people relaxing, playing, and enjoying the water. On the other side, the noisy traffic belches its pollution, and the concrete jungle of luxury high-rises stand facing the beach, with the poor neighborhoods behind them.

◉ *Nothing Shabby About Ipanema*

In many respects, life in Ipanema is similar to life in Europe or the United States.

Ipanema is a lively, clean section of Rio. It is residential but has lots of shops, cafés, movie theaters, and places to eat. It also has great places for young people to have fun on weekends. There are air-conditioned malls perfect for shopping for popular brands and meeting up with friends. People living in the oceanfront apartment buildings usually have air-conditioning in every room of their apartment.

Behind the high-rises are tree-lined lanes with magnificent villas. Most of these mansions are protected by armed guards who use the latest in sophisticated technology to watch the properties. Ipanema is a wealthy neighborhood in the heart of a South American city. With all the poverty and social injustice in Rio de Janeiro, poor people from the nearby crowded favelas (ghettos) envy Ipanema residents.

Sometimes, Marcos sees street children who eye him as he goes by. It is easy to recognize them. They walk barefoot in small groups. Their clothes are tattered and dirty. They stop motorists at red lights to wash their windshields for a few coins. Marcos's parents have warned him to be careful around street children because hunger can make anybody aggressive. Sometimes street children attack tourists or rich children. From his bedroom window, Marcos can see the hillside and its favelas. The hill is home to a poor population of mostly black families. The flimsy corrugated roofs on their houses give them little protection from bad weather.

Favelas: Home to the City's Poorest

"Favela" is a Brazilian word for "shantytown"—in other words, areas of the city where only poor people live. Unfortunately, it is a word known around the world because when the subject of Brazil comes up, its slums are usually the main topic.

Imagine: There are some five hundred favelas in Rio and its suburbs, which are home to 30 percent of the area's total population. That means four million people live in slums. Rio de Janeiro was the political capital of the country until 1960. Today, it is Brazil's tourist hub. It has, after all, kept its image as a rich, thriving city where dreams can come true. This explains why many disadvantaged people continue to move here. They hope for good luck.

Generally speaking, favelas have developed on the city hillsides that overlook the big beaches of the rich neighborhoods. The hillsides used

to have dense vegetation and were considered too steep for any buildings. Until the 1950s, there was nothing there. Then, the price for homes went sky high, and poor people started to take over the hills' vacant land, clear away trees and brush, then build their own little huts without anybody's permission. They made roofs and walls out of scrap metal and old boards because they earned next to nothing and had to survive.

The years passed. What had been hamlets with only a couple of houses (no running water and rarely any electricity) turned into towns with no real planning. Today, the crowded lanes also hold grocery stores, hardware stores, and other useful shops.

Many people in favelas make their living by doing odd jobs. Others work in small businesses. There are vendors, window washers, windshield washers, and garbage collectors. As you can imagine, they make very little money. They do not earn enough to pay for decent housing. The government has tried many social programs, but none of its solutions have worked for the decades-long problem.

Rio's favelas have long had a reputation for serious crime—so serious that the police hesitate before going into them. Drugs have plagued the slums for a very long time. For young people who do not know how to read or write, selling drugs is the easiest way to earn money. It is also the most dangerous. Police frequently burst into the favelas to break up drug rings and arrest the leaders. Sometimes at night, you can hear gunfire between gangs and the police.

Marcos says he is used to it. In Rio, it has become accepted as part of life. Marcos has even been up the hillside. There, he has seen a few positive sides to life in the favelas. He went up with a friend to visit Mangueira, one of Rio's most famous favelas. They had to climb hundreds of steps before reaching the top. Once at the top, they had a magnificent view of the city and the ocean. The ambiance in Mangueira is relaxed and fun. It is one of the rare favelas that can be visited. Most of them have well-earned reputations for being dangerous.

The boys stumble upon a group of samba guitarists playing a famous song called "A Mangueira." You might say it's the neighborhood anthem. The tune is so catchy, Marcos cannot get it out of his head. Everybody enjoys singing along. It has a carnival feel to it.

Mangueira is home to one of the most famous samba dance schools in all of Brazil. Locals come to learn to dance the samba in little schools run by associations. They sing and practice the guitar chords so that they're ready to play during carnival.

Carnival and the Samba School

"A Felicidade" ("Happiness") is a great old song that wisely says, "A poor man's joy resembles the grand illusion of carnival." Though carnival is fun, it is only costumes and make-believe.

The samba is both a type of music and a type of dance that began in Rio in the early 1900s. Once again, the origins are African. To be more precise, the samba has it roots in the traditions

and folklore of Angola. In 1915, several musicians gathered in a house in Rio. They had all left Bahia behind. Most of them were black descendants of slaves. The chemistry between them was amazing. They improvised danceable tunes with fast beats. The samba was born. It immediately became Brazil's most popular music.

The samba used to be danced by two partners. The main rule was to hold each other tight, press belly button against

belly button, and sway to the music. Today, people dance it just about any way they feel like dancing it. All it takes is following the rhythm of the drums. In terms of music, there are really two sorts of sambas: the one that you listen to at home, called *samba-canção*, which is soft, melancholic, and sad; and the *samba-enredo*, with a joyous, fast-beat tempo that people love dancing to at parties.

Every year in February, the Cariocas stop going about their usual business and enjoy Rio's gigantic carnival. Kids and grown-ups alike love it. People dress up as clowns, pirates, monsters, belly-dancers, Greek gods—you name it. Then they march down the streets, singing, dancing, and celebrating for four days. South of the equator, February is summertime. So when it's winter and freezing in Europe and North America, it's steamy and hot in Brazil.

Marcos meets up with his friends on Arpoador Beach. Surf's up! On the beach, a small group of girls is tanning not far from the boys. They are talking about the latest episode of a TV show, a *telenovela*, a type of soap opera made in Brazil.

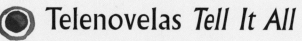

◉ Telenovelas *Tell It All*

Marcos also loves *telenovelas*, sentimental TV series that tell the story of families over a number of episodes.

The shows last fifty minutes on average and can run for up to two hundred episodes. Though the plots usually focus on dramatic, passionate twists and turns, much like American soap operas, *telenovelas* also tackle the problems of daily life, sometimes touching on serious subjects like racism, corruption, AIDS, and illiteracy. From firefighters to school principals to rich entrepreneurs, all social groups are represented.

Telenovelas project an image of modern society. For example, characters use the most sophisticated cell phones and computers, and ride in helicopters, transportation common among businesspeople in Rio de Janeiro and São Paulo.

***Telenovelas* are very popular** because everyone can relate to them. In general, they air at the end of the day, around 6 P.M. TV Globo, the major Brazilian TV network, airs three a day. Brazilians often stop what they're doing to watch their favorite shows. Each *telenovela* has its own Web page, with a discussion forum, a presentation of the actors' wardrobes, summaries of upcoming episodes, and more. Launched in the 1960s, *telenovelas* are today a veritable industry, with videos and DVDs, original sound tracks, and a multitude of other products. Many young people proudly wear T-shirts with the logo of their favorite show.